HEY. . .
MISTER BIRDMAN
A BUS DRIVER'S BIRD ADVENTURE

STOP THE BUS
I WANT TO GET
ON . . .

By Charles P. Mason

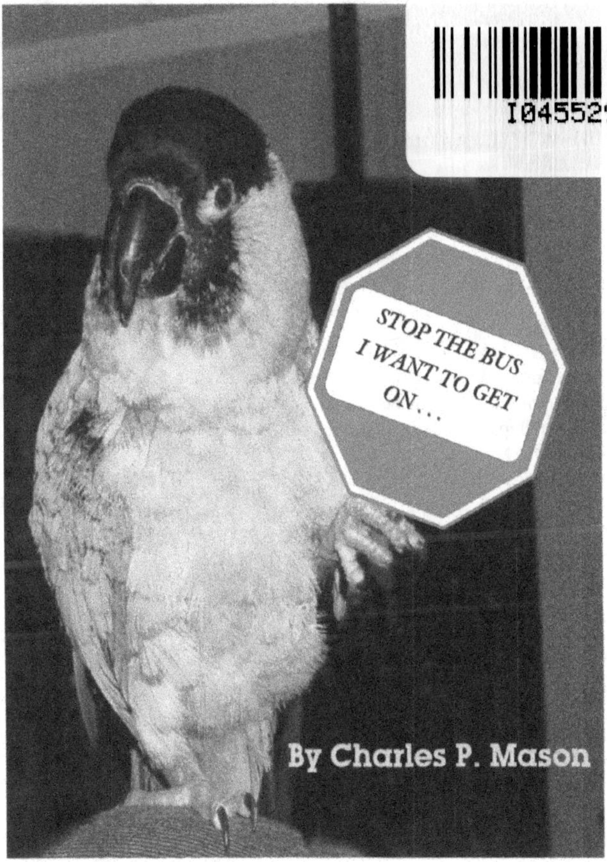

outskirtspress
DENVER, COLORADO

Hey Mister Birdman
A Bus Driver's Bird Adventure
All Rights Reserved.
Copyright © 2013 Charles P. Mason
v3.0 r1.0

Outskirts Press, Inc.
http://www.outskirtspress.com

ISBN: 978-1-4787-0641-0

Library of Congress Control Number: 2013907795

Outskirts Press and the "OP" logo are trademarks belonging to Outskirts Press, Inc.

PRINTED IN THE UNITED STATES OF AMERICA

Introduction

These short stories are for those that can enjoy one man's journey into the world of birds and how I learned a universal truth about the important glue of life. What allows us to love all or part of the different forms of life. How is it that I can love my pet and yet not love my neighbor or a so called friend?

Birds show us their lives, and like many of you I could spend hours, watching them as they fly about, doing what birds do. After putting up a bird feeder in my yard many different birds started to show up to eat the seed and I could see them close up. I guess the old saying that "If you feed them they will come," is true because shortly I had a flock at my feeder all the time. I found out that they also have close family ties with each other and will look out for one another, especially the young chicks who are trying to get their fair share of the food. From what I saw, birds set up guards to watch the flock while they all eat or sleep. I have heard it said that the family is the cornerstone of the world. I believe it's an inner structure of some kind that keeps all of us, including animals closely connected to each other. I thought about the word, family and decided to look the word up in the dictionary, just to find out what the big thinkers say the true meaning of the word family is. Their thought was that it is a group of persons sharing a common ancestry. I thought to myself, that's it…there has to be more to it than that? I believe there is more to the word "Family," than just a human biological ancestry. A family could be the binding together of friendships between people, or even between people and their pets. Many times pets become part or even all of your family. Before you can love someone or something, you first have to trust them. Birds and animals build on that trust and will only come to you after trust has been created. Birds live by either fly or they die, trust does not come easy for birds. It took years to build trust in my birds and many bites on my hands because they were not hand fed as babies. It took unending, forgiveness from me to earn their love and their trust, but it was well worth it in the end to have them as part of my family and I part of theirs.

Let me tell you about one quick story that I was watching on television. It was about a lady who had to give her horse away to an animal shelter. She couldn't keep her pet horse any longer because of the cost and she had no job. As the time grew nearer for the change of ownership of the horse, the owner started to cry. It was a sad time for her and hard to see her in such pain. Among her sobs and visible pain, she repeated these words, "He's become part of my family, and I love him. He's my only true friend, and I will never forget him." I thought about her words and came to the understanding that it wasn't the ancestry that connects us as family. It's the love through trust we have for each other and our pets. It's the trust that is the unseen true glue…that's the real binding of our feelings for each other humans and animals. Fate can bring us all together, but we have to join hands spiritually, to become a true family. Using my imagination I gave my birds a voice and wrote what I thought they were saying to show their personalities.

Table of Contents

My Lucky Bill

August 26th in Chicago is frequently very hot and dry, but 1992 was the exception. Each day brought rain and more cold rain so my leaving for work as a bus driver was becoming a real chore. I looked out the window and the late morning sun was finally trying to come out, so with a great reluctance, it was off to work driving a city bus once more. I did my morning shift and then went home for lunch. Soon it was time to return to work for the afternoon drive. As I stepped off my porch, I saw a small white bird with orange cheeks just sitting there on my lawn. He looked like he had no cares in the world and wasn't even moving a feather. For about a minute, we just stared at each other and finally I called to him with the usual soft hellos. Then I slowly walked towards him and he still didn't move. He had this very tall yellow crest of hair standing straight up from the top of his head. He looked like a real palace guard standing there, all stiff and at attention.

Gently I knelt down next to him with my index finger stretched out, and he took two quick jumps right onto my finger. I don't know who was more surprised him, or me. With that, he started walking right up my uniform sleeve all the way up to the top of my shoulder, and then he just sat there like he was my old, long lost friend. As we checked each other out, he seemed right at home on my shoulder but then he did what all birds do, he pooped! All over my clean bus drivers uniform sleeve.

And I might say, with complete and total disregard for the importance of what he had just messed up. He had great aim because he also pooped on my bus drivers arm patch with my official employee numbers on it. I'm sure he saw the shock on my face, but he just sat there staring at me wearing this little sly look on his face. In my mind, I could almost hear him say, *Well that's what we little birds do, eat'n poop, poop'n eat and sometimes, I just fly around a bit!* This I thought was kind of pushy for a guy who just showed up on my doorstep at the last minute! Not knowing what to do with this bird, I decided to bring him into the house where it would be safe and warm until my wife or I got home that night.

When I got to work I told one of the drivers about the strange thing that had just happened to me on my lunch hour. He said, "If a bird stops at your house and poops on you, it's for sure a good omen, a sign of good luck. Go out and buy a Lotto ticket for tonight." Something inside me said, this is just another one of those many old wives tales you hear about from your local fortuneteller, but you never really know for sure. I took the chance anyway and rushed out to buy my lucky lottery ticket.

As I drove my bus around on my route that night I thought, he's only a bird, a very small one no less, but still, what if? When the time came for them to pick the numbers on the radio, I almost couldn't wait. Well you guessed it, nothing, only two of my numbers out of all the numbers picked and I needed six to win. Well so much for all those, big time omens and the old worldly folk tales. All I knew was I didn't win!

The next morning, as I drove my bus along my route, one of my regular passengers leaned over to me and said. "Did you know that your numbers came in last night and the ticket was worth five thousand dollars?" I told her only two of my numbers in the big lotto came in last night. She replied "No, the numbers on your sleeve in the Pick Four Lotto, you know you're I. D. patch numbers, 7091, those numbers won big time." "Oh no," I said to her, "I played the wrong lotto, I bought the big Lotto, not the pick four Lotto." As I drove along, I told her the story about the bird and what he had done on my sleeve and arm patch. Well she started laughing out loud and said, " What more could the little guy do to show you what numbers to pick, point his wing down to the lucky numbers and say! Here, right here, look at the blue numbers on your patch." It was 1,0,7,9 in the little pick four numbers Lotto, not the big one. I really felt like Mr. Fool then, after all he had marked the spot. Well, anyway, I might not have won the big Lotto, but I feel it was lucky we found Bill that day, as he would have died out there in the cold rain. He also had no fear of other animals so they would have gotten him. We waited for a few short weeks and finding no lost and found ads or calls to the police station, we felt that the bird was ours to keep.

Soon we were off to the bird doctor and then to the pet store for a good cage and some food for our new bird. You know the proper kind of food that only healthy birds like to eat. Later on I found out that whatever is on my plate is good enough for him.

Sometimes it's a battle as to who gets to the potatoes first. As for his favorite snack, it's pasta, so you better look out because he tries to grab the long ones before you can get to them. I think he believes they are real worms.

At the pet doctor's office, we found out that he was a male Lutino Cockatiel. Ah yes it was a boy bird, I was so happy. I wanted to break out singing, "My Boy Bill" from the stage show Carousel.

Now that he had a name we went about gathering all those goodies for Bill. We soon started to feel like many new grandparents, quickly buying everything in sight. Price was no object, not for our boy, Bill. I tell you, this bird really had it made in the shade. I found that these little birds will really melt you down no matter how big you think you are!

When you read the various bird magazines, you find that you are not alone in this deep infatuation brought on by being a new bird owner. So you buy, buy and then buy some more. At least until most of the money, runs out. We heard many stories from owners telling us all the cute and unusual things their birds do to amuse them. I find the high intelligence of some birds is astounding. After I've taped Bill with the video camera and then replayed it back, he knows he is seeing himself on our television set. He even chirps back at the set when he hears himself or other birds. It's time for us all to drop the old term, "It's just a dumb bird."

I'm sure I bored a lot of people to death with

my long stories and then with all those photos I had taken of Bill, you know my guy from every possible angle. Was I on my way to being hooked? You bet! To my wife and me, there's a whole new fraternity of bird loving people out there, just waiting for us to meet them. Now, when people board my bus, it's not how are you Chuck, it's "how's Bill?" I think they're getting hooked too.

An unusual thing happened as we were trying to understand this new bird in our lives. One day we noticed that, when we came home, Bill was always and I mean always, on the corner of the couch calmly sitting on the quilt that my wife's mother had made for us many years ago. It was a beauty, all covered with a floral pattern and when we tried to take him off the quilt, he would begin attacking us.

We started to wonder what was going on in this little guy's mind. I'd done nothing to upset him and there he was, biting at my finger with a cross look on his face. When we finally got him off the blanket even to fold it, he flew right back to it. He only wanted to stay there on the quilt. After days of thought, we figured it out. He was protecting the flowers printed on the backing of grandma's quilt. I guess he thought it was his nest. If we didn't do something about it, the homemade quilt would soon be covered all over with many of Bills gifts. This I knew would not be very well appreciated by my wife or grandma.

So it was off to the fabric store for some flowered cloth. If you can, imagine a very large six foot two man just walking around in a fabric store, checking the many different materials to see if the flowers were just right for Bill, that is. Quickly and without fuss I wandered all over the store knowing that the sales ladies were trying to decide who was going to ask this strange guy if he needed any help. Finally, one young lady came over and asked if she could help me find anything special and just what I needed the fabric for. I replied, "No, I was just looking for a small piece of flowered cloth for my bird." Well, I don't want to tell you about the look on her face as she thought they had a very big nut roaming about in the store. She just nodded slowly and said ok, and went back to the others smiling all the way. I found a pattern with some small flowers on it and everyone was happy when I left. When I got home, Bill was in his cage eating away and didn't even notice me remove the quilt away and exchange it for the new piece of cloth on the couch

Soon he was out running across the top of the couch and when he saw the new cloth he stopped dead in his tracks, staring at it for the longest time. You could tell from the expression on his face, he knew this was not the same cloth! Bill leaned over the side of the arm to see if grandma's special quilt was maybe stored down on the floor, but it wasn't. I could see from his face he was giving this a lot of deep thought, he then looked back at the new cloth and finally after many looks, he decided the new one was his to keep. Bill has been happy as a lark ever since.

We thought our new bird should have another physical because he was still new to us. After seeing the doctor, he told us that a healthy bird like Bill might leave about forty-two "gifts" (If you know what I mean,) around the house for us each day. Well Bill from the time we got him until now, has been very, very generous with his gifts. As I'm his special friend, he gives me extra gifts. That's why I decided to refer to him on occasions as, Bill the Poop or The Duke of Poop." He came to us as a free flying bird and we felt that he should stay that way and free to fly. So he has the run of the house. Armed with my roll of toilet tissue, I explore the rooms to see where he has been. I'm now considered a member in good standing of the "Royal Order of the Poop Patrol."

I think about Bill as I drive my bus around and I can remember when I bought him a new gym set for his cage. I tried to put him on the swinging perch thinking that he would have a lot of fun, but he just fell off, twice in fact, flat on his beak. Then he gave me a look, twice okay, but a third time… no way! Playing on the gym set was not to be in Bills future because he never used it.

The thing that was a real eye opener to me was this fascination Bill had for our feet. He just seemed to like feet.

When we're sitting with our feet up on the couch, he would come up to them real close and just start to chirp away at them. He would climb up on my toes and I'd begin to move my toes up and down, then back and forth. No matter how I moved them, he would just hang on with both feet. He looked like a little cowboy riding the mechanical bull at the local bar. You could almost hear him shouting "*Yeee Haaaaa*" as he hung on tight to this bucking bull. When I stopped, he would peck at my toes until I started up again. Well, that seemed like a lot of fun for Bill, but because of his sharp nails my toes started to hurt, even though I wore stockings on my feet. One day I called home and my wife said. "Bill has a big surprise for you when you get home, and it's about your feet."

That night I put my feet up and Bill saddled up onto my toes and we started, his head arched back as he went around on his private bull. Then it happened, I could see from his face that the usual, *"Yeee Haaa's"* had suddenly changed To *Ooooo Yeah, Oh Yeah!* My wife was right about the surprise, Bill thought that my foot was a girl bird and he was, making mad passionate love to some girly toes. How do you like that! So when he spots my feet, he thinks it's his time for some quick pleasure. *"Oh, Nooooo,"* I say to him, I have a headache, little man" and I put my feet down flat on the floor. So now he only sings softly, while he's dancing around next to my feet just tweeting away. Bill brings a new smile to our hearts each time we see him do things like dance to his favorite country songs, bobbing his head and patting his feet up and down to the music.

He reminds me of our teenagers, they never listened to the words either, just the strong beat. I can even make tap dancing sounds with my mouth and he's off running over to me and joins in with me on my shoulder. It's great watching the inner curiosity he has when he tries something new. When he's not really too sure because of a strange sound in the room it's up to my shoulder for some protection.

During the first Christmas season Bill was with us, our coming and going seemed normal to him until we put up the tree. He watched as we put on all the Christmas lights, sparkling garland and ornaments in place. The tree was coming alive with holiday spirit but he kept his distance, not quite sure what this was all about. We went out one night to buy something and when we came back, Bill was nowhere to be found. We both started to panic about Bill, just where he could be. We kept calling for him as we went all around the house. We looked under, on top and inside of just about every place he could be. Soon we thought that maybe Bill had gotten out of the house as we were going out the door. This was serious, so we went all over the living room again and again. I was on the floor looking under the couch, when my wife said. "Hey Chuck, look at who's in the Christmas tree."

There he was quietly sitting on one of the tree branches, surrounded by the many ornaments, just watching me roll around on the floor looking for him. He never made a sound even when we were calling "Hey Bill, Hey Bill." All he knew was that he was contented just being where he was, next to some fake bird ornaments among the tree and watching us as we went around the room, and me rolling around on the floor. My wife went over to the tree and got him from where he was sitting and Bill was all smiles, I guess he was laughing and just wanted to be part of the Christmas events.

Each morning when my wife is in the kitchen, there's Bill, walking all around at her feet just singing away and whistling. Sometimes I think, he's telling her all about the dreams he had the night before. He must have had some good one's because he'd talk for at least fifteen minutes, and my wife would answer back to him, "Is that right Bill or no kidding Bill" I always thought it was kind of odd, whenever I would see people talking out loud to their pets. It was as though their pets were just another person in the over-all conversation. The nice thing is our pets just sit there and listen and many times you wonder if they really do understand you. Lately I even find myself doing it to, just talking away like my pet really understood me. I guess it's because they don't talk back to us that makes it good for our souls. We feel that Bill, was our gift from God and he brings much happiness to us each day with his calming presence. Whenever I'm down in the dumps, and the world has left me behind, Bill helps me back up. Was it luck or fate that placed Bill on our lawn that day? Who knows, but when I see him flying towards me, all I know is I'm happy, the stress of the day just melts away. I believe that pets become reflections of our-selves. I have always felt that if you look deep enough into their eyes, you will see the common bonds between all of life, and how we really do need each other. And when we lose them…well you know. What else can I say except, little Bill is small, but oh my.

Good crow ... bad crow

Have you ever been awake early morning and hear the blackbirds or crows, barking their caw, caw sounds? They seem to be sending messages back and forth to each other as they hunt for food. Blackbirds and crows look for just about anything to feed on, from road kill to robbing nests of baby chicks.

I start to work each morning about sunrise and get to see many beautiful skies and colors every day. But, along with the sunrises I see many animals digging for food or gathering berries off the trees. I also see the many crows gathering together like wolf packs getting ready for the food hunt of the day. One morning as I was pulling my bus out of the driveway, there in the middle of the driveway was one of many songbirds that use the bus barn as a nesting place. I stopped my bus and just watched her. Soon she flew away and there on the ground was this small chick. It must have been hiding for safety under its mom.

Soon the mother came back and covered over the chick to protect it. This went on for a few minutes but the two were in the way of all our buses and both were sure to get ran over by one of our buses pulling out.

When the mother left, I picked up the chick to save it from certain death and placed it safely into the next lot. It was empty and had some tall weeds that the chick could hide in until the mother got back. Soon she came looking for the chick and the chick seeing her, made some noises and the mother went to it and the feeding continued, and I moved on. When I came back at about noon, there they still were in the next parking lot. All was safe and both seemed happy. I could see the little chick peeking out from under its mom's feathers. The next morning when I started back to work, I parked my car in the empty lot where the two birds were. The sun had just come up above the trees, and the bright sun was hitting the many leaves, making them shine brightly. I looked around and there was the chick, all by itself and in the middle of that big open lot. This, I thought, was kind of dangerous so I picked up the chick and placed it back into the weeds and out of sight. When the mother came back, she had no trouble finding the little bird. But, there was trouble in the air and it came in the form of a flock of crows. They were out for the morning hunt and I think they spotted the feeding session that was going on between the mother bird and her chick. The mother came out of the weeds and tried to play hurt as she moved away from where the chick was hiding. I guess she told the chick to stay inside the weeds because it never came out. The crows I think knew better, she wasn't hurt, she was hiding something. The crows numbered about four and only one mother. They each went to different places around the lot as they called out signals to each other. One crow would swoop down to see if there was a chick, and then the mother would attack that crow even though she was much smaller.

The crows knew that I was there since I also made my presence known to them, so the crows soon flew away. It was almost time for me to report for work so I had to leave the two of them there alone in the lot. It was so hard because I was torn between staying with the two birds to protect them, or going to do my job on time?

The job won because it would be difficult to explain to my boss why I didn't show up that day. With a heavy heart, I went on into work. All morning I couldn't get the mother and the baby chick out of my mind. The hours went by so slowly I could hardly stand it. I told myself that they were going to be all right, and that they would manage fine without my help. After all, I can't play God.

When I returned to my car after my morning shift, I hurried over to the empty lot where I had left them, but I couldn't find the chick or its mother anywhere. Soon the mother showed up, chirping for the chick to come out. She looked frantically around the lot, but still no chick. We both stood there for a very long time staring at each other. I knew she knew my thoughts, as well as I knew hers. The chick was gone. My eyes started to well up with tears and all I could think of was *those bums. Those pieces of slime, they came back and took the chick!* They outsmarted me and only went away for a short time, or at least until I was gone, and then came back to fight it out with the mother over the chick. All I could do after that was walk around in circles, weeping softly about the fate of the chick. Over and over in my mind I called those crows every bad think I knew. I hoped that someday they would get theirs…like, starting right now. Shortly, the mother bird flew away, and I got into my car and went on home. Tears filled my eyes as I drove home. When I got home, my face must have shown that I was under a lot of stress and something was horrible wrong.

"What's wrong honey?" my wife asked. I guess our faces are like road maps, every inch, out there for all to read. "Nothing I replied … it's nothing, I just want to be left alone." Well, if you have a wife like mine that just won't work. I went and sat down on the couch and she came and sat down next to me. I started to really sob then, as I put my head down in my hands near my knees. At the same time, all I could do was say, "Those dirty rats ate my chick." I kept saying that over and over, still sobbing as I tried to get the words out. "Who?" my wife asked again and again?

Suddenly I cried out, "Those no good, dirty crows, they came back and grabbed the chick I was watching at the barn. They just came back and stole the chick from the mother when she was away and tore it apart and ate it." All that I could think of was the total terror that the chick must have felt as the crow's descended down upon it. One of them snatching it up in its beak and then all of them fighting over its precious body parts as the chick screamed for its mom. I became what some people would call, *a basket case,* about this whole matter. My heavy sobbing went on for a good part of an hour and all my wife could do was hold me close to her. While this was going on, Bill sat on my shoulder trying to figure out what was making me so sad. Then he did the most precious thing I can remember, he reached around from my shoulder where he was perched and licked a single tear that was running down my cheek, as though saying, *It's all right dad. You did your best.* All I could say was *"Oh, Bill, oh, Bill you are so good."*

That afternoon was about as hard on me as the time we had to put our female collie dog to sleep because she had epilepsy seizures and was in pain. The doctor said it was for the best. For my family, it was days and days of deep sorrow. If you are reading this story, I'll bet you've had to suffer through much of the same inner pain yourself, when you lose a pet. All I knew is, it's hard.

I went back to work that afternoon and my eyes were still glazed over with tears. One rider asked if I was all right and I replied, "yes, it's some pollen I got in my eyes and can't seem to get it out." Weeks went by and as you all know, time heals almost all wounds. Ah yes, it was now Friday morning, my favorite day of the week. As I slowly drove out of the shopping mall, there in the oncoming traffic side. I saw a small crow resting in the street. After a closer look, I could see that it was hurt and not moving at all just turning its head from side to side. It might have been hit and stunned by a moving car, so I slowly pulled my bus up next to the crow. It still just sat there not moving at all, just looking around like everything was okay, but the crow was facing the oncoming traffic, and it could plainly see the cars as the cars passed by, and it still didn't move.

The crow had no idea that in less than a minute, it was going to be just another piece of road kill and I hated that because I would have to see it all day as it was run over and over again until it was flat like a rag on the street. Without giving it a second thought, I parked my bus and got off. I went over to the small crow and picked it up. Next I placed the bird on the grass next to some bushes, safely out of the way. This way I felt it could gain its thoughts back, without getting run over by a car. Other crows were nearby and were having a fit about my picking up the bird and putting it on the grass. Some of my bus passengers were also wondering where the heck I had gone to in such a hurry. It looked to them, like I had flown off the bus like a gazelle. As I picked up the young crow, I could see that some passengers were most likely thinking to themselves. *Don't touch that filthy thing you never know what kind of germs it has.* Oh well, I did it anyway and I'm still here and my fingers still haven't fallen off yet.

I felt pretty good about what I had just done. But, in the back of my mind there was this voice saying to me. *Hey I thought you couldn't wait for the crows to get theirs, you know after what they did to your chick and all. Now you went off the bus and you wimped out. You had your big chance to see a crow get his, and you missed it!* I thought it over and asked myself are there good crows or are they all bad crows? Who am I to judge them? After all they were doing what crows do, just like all the other animals in the food chain. But still it hurts to think that, that's what the wild is all about. Even hunters at times become the hunted. I myself do all my food hunting at the food marts: I never want to meet what I eat, as the saying goes. However, if I had to live in the wild, I too would have to learn to adapt.

Getting back to the small crow, I looked for him when I came by about one hour later and there he was, still sitting by the bushes where I had placed him. The next morning when I came by, he was still sitting there, he hadn't moved. I thought that on my next pass by, I would get a box along the way and put the crow into it. I covered him so he couldn't get out and that way no one knew he was inside the box as I drove along, Later on I would take him to my vet.

A friend came onto my bus and she asked, "What's in the box?" I answered, "I have a live crow inside." She laughed and blurted out, "No way, where did you get that story?" Well, you could have blown her over with a feather when

I opened the box and she could see the crow sitting in there. After a lot of discussion about the crow, she said, "I'll take the crow to your vet for you if it will help. I know you're still on duty and can't go." I knew then that for the crow, the lifeboats were on the way!

So off to the doctor they both went, and I'm sure the crow had no idea what was going on or where he was going. A day ago he was in the street and now he's taking a bus ride. Was this something or what! After that, I felt confident that all would be okay once she got the crow to the vet's office. When she got there, the nurse said she would take care of the crow, not to worry. Later, my friend got back on the bus and said she felt much better about the whole thing. Later that afternoon I called the vet's office and asked how the crow was. I was coldly told that it had already been put to sleep! I stood at the phone speechless. In a rage I asked, "What happened that you had to kill the crow, he looked fine?" The nurse said that the crow's legs had not grown like they should have, and it would never survive in the wild so it had to be destroyed. She told me that they get a lot of birds in there that can't make it in the wild, so they are also destroyed.

I really felt sick after that because my friend and I went through all that trouble thinking the bird would get the help of my vet, and get better, not just be killed. I guess when you work with as many animals each day as they do, one common crow wouldn't matter much. The nurse at that animal hospital should have had some caring left in her voice, when people call and are looking for some hope. I know this is not a prime example of those who take care of our animals but I felt she gave me as some would say, the short and sweet of it all. When we brought our dog in for an exam, I asked our doctor about the crow, and asked if he really did see the crow, or was I getting the fast shuffle by the nurse. I told him, "When I called and asked before, I was told by another nurse that you, yourself saw the small crow. I just had to know?" In conversation, he said that he had seen the bird and that crows are his favorite wild birds. He also told me that crows maintain a very close family bond with each other and will tend to one of their own when it gets sick or can't get food for itself. They will also gather up water and food in their beaks and bring it back to the nest for the sick crow to eat and drink. So I guess there are good crows as well as bad crows, it all depends on what they're doing at the time you see them.

The new guy on the block

Tick-tock, tick-tock, time marches on and we have had Bill with us for two years now, and he has been at my side like we were stuck in glue. Oh, what a happy feeling. When I was at home we went everywhere together and I mean everywhere even to taking my showers, he was there watching me bathe. From the look on his face, it was as if he was wondering just how, could dad take off all of his feathers, one at a time? Then climb into that big water hole looking like a plucked chicken, and after that, then put all new feathers back on him-self, plus change all their colors to. Now Bill doesn't like splashing in water, so we squirt him with a squeeze bottle and that he likes. When he's up on the shower door rail and you can mist him with water spray, he will spread his wings out like he's flying, and we call this, Bill's Eagle Man pose, and it's my favorite. One day at the lunch table we were enjoying my sandwich together the phone rang, it was our banker returning my call. As we talked Bill made some whistling noises and the banker asked. "Do you have a bird there?" "Oh, you heard him?" I said. "That's my boy Bill, he's a small cockatiel that just showed up at our place one day and has been with us ever since." Like I said before, all that a bird lover has to hear is the magic question. "Do you have a bird?" For sure, he's in for one of those long, ten-minute speeches. When I finally got all talked out about Bill, he asked, "Do you want another bird? My wife and children hate my bird because of its size and he screams very loud. When they try to touch him, he screams and bites at them, so no one can ever come close to him, except me. I had him in college so he knows and likes only me and he's not at all happy with anyone else." *Hmmm another bird, what to do with another bird I thought?* To have two birds and a dog might be pushing the wife a little too much, but I had to ask anyway what kind of bird it was. "He's a Nanday Conure," he told me. "Sort of like a small parrot with lots of green and blue feathers. To top it off, he has a black crown on the top of his head and a real big black beak. But best of all, this guy has some neat red socks on his legs, which make him a real stand out guy. Like I said before, I have to get rid of him because my wife and kids don't get along with Brutus."

Uh- oh, his name should have given me a clue. Brutus probably had a one track mind of his own. But maybe that's not so bad, we all have feelings from time to time. I told him I'd look around to see if I could find Brutus a good home.

That evening, I called my daughter Dorothy, about the bird and she suggested I call our dentist friend because he had three kids and just maybe they would like the bird. So I made the call, I asked him if he would like a bird? His reply was. "Funny you should ask, the kids and I were going out tonight, to look for a pet bird, what kind of bird is it?" With that, I said, "I'll make you an offer you just can't refuse. For only ten bucks you get a bird, a cage, and some food, and how could you pass that up." "Sounds good" he said, let's take a look at him and see what happens. If my wife and kids like him, it's a deal." I called the banker back to make the arrangements and that night we were to take this guy called Brutus, over to what was to be his new home.

At the banker's house, I met Brutus. Oh boy, there he was clinging to the inside bars of his cage, watching me like a hawk. I realized that with this guy, it was going to be a real test of wills … his, against mine. His eyes were open wide and on me as I moved towards him. Then it happened, he opened his beak and started to emit some very, very ear-piercing screeches. *Wow, this loud of a sound, could not possibly be made by such a small bird.* Those sounds must have started way deep down in his toes and grew in volume until they came out of his beak.

Ack!-Ack! On and on he went. My little bird Bill never, ever, made that loud of a noise, not even when he was really mad at me, so I moved back. Brutus's green and blue tail feathers were half beaten off. I could see in his eyes that it was going to take a lot more than just a little tender loving care to cope with this new guy. It was clear to me he was not a very happy camper. Slowly, we covered the cage and Brutus quieted down. Then it was off to my friend, the dentists. With the new guy safe and sound in his cage, I now felt good about the whole thing. When we got to the dentist's house, everyone was excited and the kids couldn't wait to meet their new pet. They cried loudly, "Let us see him, Let us see the new bird". It was like Christmas in July. We found a place near the dining room door to place the cage and I slowly uncovered him. There was silence in the room as they got their first look at their new bird. He was still clinging to the side of his cage. You could see him trying to figure out, *who are all these people any way and what do they want from me?* For a long time, we stared at him and he stared back at us, and no one moved. Whenever anyone came near the cage, he would wake the dead with his ear piercing screams, so we all stayed well back and everything became quiet again. I don't know whose eyes were bigger, his or ours.

We made small talk for a while, and I could feel my dentist friend was not too sure about this guy called Brutus. So I told him, "It might take some time to adjust to each other, but if the bird doesn't work out, I'll take him back. My guarantee to you is as good as gold, and you could take that to the bank!" My banker friend had to go so he wished us all well and I said good night.

I knew if you ever had a pet for ten long years, it would be hard to leave it behind, so the less we said, the better.

Three days later, I called our dentist friend to ask how Brutus and everyone was getting along? The answer was. "Not so good, I and the kids were sort of looking for something we could all hold and cuddle, like a small cat maybe. All this bird does is scream at me and scare everyone to death all the time. He just clings to the side of his cage and won't let anyone near him without trying to bite you. He's really not much fun." Hearing that, I reminded him of my pledge and said I would come and take Brutus back, and do it that night, no problem. Sooo, I went quickly to the phone and using my best sheepish voice I called my daughter and said. "Hello Dorothy, how would you like a bird, a cage and all the bird stuff you could ever ask for?" My daughter's reply was, "okay I'll take him." *Yes! Yes! I thought to myself. I knew that if I put that pleading preachers warble in my voice, I'd get her to say yes, it never fails.*

With some concern in her voice, she said, "okay, but from what I've heard of Brutus, he needs a new name. I don't like the name of Brutus, it sounds too macho to me." Hmmm! A new name, what to call this new guy. Finally after many names, Dorothy decided on the name Gonzo, because he looked like one of the hand puppets birds on a television show. He had these big wide eyes peering out from just above his long black beak. He was a strange looking puppet and kind of a sad looking one at that.

So all agreed Gonzo it was, even though I thought he should have been named Long John Silver. Because, he looked to me like he should belong to a pirate, siting up high on his shoulder. His wings were kind of lopsided and his feathers looked as though he had gotten caught in a spinning clothes dryer because they were all going in different directions. His cage was too small for him now and that was the cause of his broken feathers. He had this look on his face as though he was saying, *don't you touch me, I bite, real hard!* Yet, his eyes said, *I'm a sad bird and I really want to be cuddled and loved. Only, just give me a little time.* Like I said before, if you just take some time to really look squarely into the eyes of any living thing, the eyes will tell you their hidden truths but only if you meet them on a one to one basis and not, as a threat.

The next day we all went off to the bird store like it was when we first got our bird Bill. Again, price didn't matter. Cost, what's that? Gonzo needed a new larger cage, and all that good stuff that a new pet bird needed. Armed with all the bird stuff, we went to Dorothy's house where we put it all together for him, Gonzo seeing his new home was not too sure of what really was going on You could almost feel the tension in the air.

Soon I said to Gonzo, "The time has come my friend. It's time for your big move." He knew something was coming up and real soon. I was afraid that I might get bitten, so I slowly put on one of my black leather gloves to get Gonzo out of his old cage and into his newer, much larger cage. I thought that he was ready to come out, but he wanted no part of it! You would think that Gonzo would be happy about all the new attention he was getting, but still he wanted no part of it, especially being picked up by my big black winter glove.

After a lot of thrashing around, loud screaming and much finger biting, I managed to move

Gonzo into his new home. He stayed there in his cage for about three days. He could have just walked out on his own, any time he wished to, because the cage door was wide open for him most of the time. We even built a patio for him to walk on next to his door and by he's ladder. But, no way, he stayed right there inside the cage, like a bug in a rug at Dorothy's house. Finally, we decided to take Gonzo out ourselves and put him on the floor for some exercise. Once again, it was a war of wills, his against ours, but we won this time. Only with the help of the Mighty Gloved Hand did Gonzo find himself down on the carpet. I think the carpet was a place he had not been since he was a very young bird. All he would do was look wide eyed at everything around the room. We were afraid he might fly into something and get hurt, so we all kept a close watch over him.

Slowly, he started to try and walk. He took two steps and fell down right on his face. It's a good thing he had that long beak to stop his fall. He then got up and did it again and then again, at least he was trying to walk. He only wanted to get back into his cage. Each time he got up he would reach down with his beak and pick up his right leg. Grabbing onto a stainless steel ring that went around his ankle he would lift his leg up high. It seemed to bother him as I knew it would have bothered me if I had to ware that metal ring around my leg ankle. I understand breeders put these metal rings on their birds leg's as a code. The ring, I was told later, was the way breeders knew when birds were bought or sold, if they had been hand-fed or not. I would think that the metal ring should have come off after the sale of a bird, but stores don't seem to do that. Ten years I felt was long enough for him to have this band on. Besides slavery is dead at our house, so the metal ring was soon to be, history!

We called our vet to get a complete physical for Gonzo and to have the ring cut off his leg. My wife and I were told by the doctor that Gonzo, at one time had broken, both of his wings. It must have happened some time in his past. Later, we found out from the banker that because of his family, Gonzo was first placed in the living room. Later, he was moved to the den and finally stuck down in the furnace room all by himself.

What a lonely boy. We thought about it for a while, and realized that his wings were broken at the banker's house in that small cage one night most likely in a fearful thrashing fit. When the furnace flames come on and the sounds it made, he didn't know what it was and it scared him. It's what some call, "Night Fright." I guess, he tried to fly away, but he was still locked inside his small cage, and his wings got badly broken. Without proper attention the wings healed back, but not properly. Because of his broken wings, Gonzo would never fly again so he had now become a grounded bird. The vet said, 'that birds must keep any illness or problems hidden from others to stay alive, that way other animals will not eat them. When they are sick or injured they are easy prey for other animals that are looking for food so they keep it to themselves." Nobody had much to do with Gonzo then, so his broken wings were never really noticed. He was really an unwanted bird that just sat all by himself except, for when his cage was cleaned or his water and food, were changed.

Fear not, today our Gonzo is now a very happy and becoming a more loveable bird. The doctor examined around on Gonzos body and told us he had the chest muscles of Arnold you know who and was built like the Terminator. The doctor gave him a clean bill of health so we were all very happy. Later that year, Dorothy moved back home with us to finish college, so it was yet another move for Gonzo.

We were all, going to be one big happy family again, Gonzo included. Each day Bill would fly over to Gonzos cage and walk around on the top of the cage, chirping to Gonzo. I think he was trying to make friends even though they were each different kinds of birds. Gonzo would climb over to bite at Bill's feet from inside the cage, but Bill was too fast for him. I believe there was some kind of communication going on because, a few days later, there was Bill sitting inside Gonzos cage, just taking away to Gonzo. I guess Bill just plain wore him down with all that non-stop talking, Bill, just loves to bird talk. The two have become friends and now they are like two close brothers, side by side always.

At bedtime, Gonzo would stand on his perch and spread himself out as wide as he could in front of Bill, trying to hide him from us when it was time to go to their separate cages. Bill lived in the front room and Gonzo slept in Dorothy's back bedroom. After getting Bill away from Gonzo to take him back to his own cage, I would place Bill on my shoulder, his favorite spot, but only when he wasn't with his new friend, Gonzo. I said to Bill one night, "Hey Bill, your spending more time with Gonzo, then you are with me." Bill looked at me and I could almost hear him say, *Dad, he's a bird like me, and you're not and beside he needs me more.* I gave those thoughts in my mind, some time to sink in and that made good sense to me. All I did then was just smile as he stepped off my finger onto his perch, and I wished him good night. Bill was one good guy. Each day they were both on top of Gonzos cage and Bill would launch himself off the cage and fly into the air, all around the room. I could almost hear Bill saying, *Come on Gonzo, let's fly, let's fly, its simple give it a try.* He did this several times and then Gonzo finally went over to the edge of the cage. All was silent as Gonzo tried flapping his wings up and down, but they never had the power to lift him into the air, no matter how many times he tried. He gave it lots of effort, but it always was a no go. Even on the floor, he could only try as he hopped around the floor, wings just a flapping away. The good thing about his trying to fly was that his shoulders got a real good workout. Bill soon figured out that Gonzo couldn't fly, he could only walk around and not so good even at that. Each day Bill would walk around on the floor with him and slowly Gonzo got much better at walking.

Free of the cage, he really progressed in his body movements and just plain moved fast across the floor. Gonzo waddles as he runs and still not as fast as Bill but he tries, now Bill, he's fast. Gonzo is slowly getting to be one good and happy guy. I think it's because of all the love that he gets from all of us. Lately, Gonzo just likes to strut around the house exploring his new space. He and Bill seem to know when it's time for bed, and they both walk down the long hall together to Gonzos cage in the back bedroom. They look like two old friends out for an evening stroll. Gonzos body clock has his bedtime worked out almost to the minute. Just how he knows this is a mystery to us. He starts screaming his ack … ack'n song about 8:25 P.M. And he doesn't stop screaming until we all come back and tuck him in. When Gonzo starts his alarm sounds, it's telling us it's time for his bed, no if's and's or but's. Often we're all in the front room watching television at that time and it's now sleepy time, so we put Bill and Gonzo on our shoulders and walk down the hallway singing the off to bed Grand March song to the music of a circus march. The Grand March song goes something like this. "It's Gonzos beddie bye time, it's Gonzos beddie bye time, it's time to say good night, cause everything's all right, it's time to say ado because the day's all through." The song goes on for a few more stanzas and we all seem to enjoy the Grand March back to the back bedroom. As we walk down the hall with them on our shoulders, Bill starts to bob his head up and down while Gonzo leans far forward and tries to look like the big eagle on the post office wall. (I think he feels that he's really flying.) I know this sounds kind of odd for two grown adults to be doing the bedtime march, but even I get to enjoy the long walk back to Gonzos cage. Oh, well, when you become a bird person, you do a lot of strange things.

We found out that Gonzo likes to drink grape

juice, and not just any kind of grape juice. It has to be only a name brand and no other. One night, the vending machine ran out of his brand so I thought I'd try one of the other brands that were now in the vending machine. He tasted it and he just walked away and I could almost hear him say. *What kind of slop is this! Me drink that, no way!* So the next day I bought the right brand of grape juice and everyone was happy. I think our birds think they are part of the rich and famous. The only problem to his drinking the grape juice is that he pooped purple … and I mean real purple!

The Sparrow

Being a bird person now, I feed some sparrows at the bus barn and also at the airport each day. The sparrows get to know when I'm coming by and all sit on the overhead rails waiting for me. If I don't get off my bus quickly after everyone is on, the birds will hop over to the open bus door and wait until I do get off and feed them all. Even my passengers enjoy watching the sparrows as they eat the seed. I find it has been a very fulfilling thing to do, and the passengers look forward to the feedings. If I'm not there that day, the passengers all tell me the next day how the birds were looking for me. Some will even give up part of their lunch, and throw out some of their sandwich bread for the birds. It seems that if you take an interest in birds, people will think you are an expert and that you know all there is to know about our flying friends. One day, after I returned from my morning bus route, the dispatcher said he had a large box which one of our drivers gave him for me when I got in. I knew this wasn't a Christmas gift since the temperature was hot outside and nearing a hundred degrees. *Hmmm! What could it be?* When I got the box, there was a note stuck on the outside and it read. *Found this bird on the garage floor, too young to fly...didn't know what to do with it. You're the Birdman, so here it is,* signed Mike. I opened the box, looked inside and saw what looked like a dead sparrow chick, but then there were some very small movements from the chick. So I knew it was still alive. I got some water in my hand and placed a few drops onto its beak with my finger. The chick responded well to the fresh water. Soon it was moving around in the box and was probably very hungry.

I headed for home where my wife, Fay mixed up some baby cockatiel food we had from Bill. I never have done anything like this before so my wife and I were all thumbs but, to the sparrow it didn't matter. It was all good stuff and she gobbled it all down. We tried feeding her with a small eye dropper, but we found in a corner store, a frozen slushy drink straw with a small spoon on one end, worked just fine.

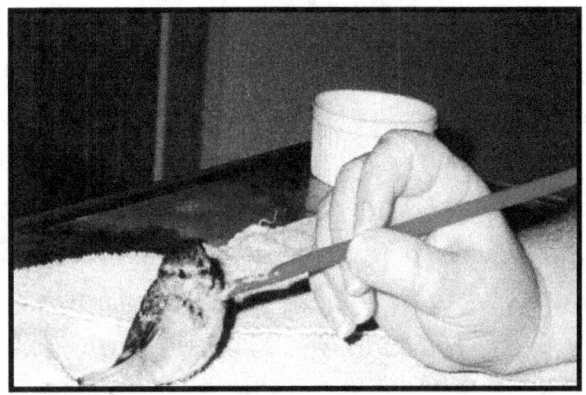

She would run from one end of the box to the other end, flapping her little wings and having a grand old time as she ate. We were really enjoying every moment as we watched her get stronger and stronger each day. While we were feeding and taking care of the sparrow, Gonzo and Bill watched with great interest. As we went about taking care of the sparrow, Bill seemed to take it all right, but Gonzo, he wasn't too sure what all this would do to his place in our house. After all he was bigger than Bill, so he thought he was the Alfa male here. I could only imagine what was going through both their minds as they looked at the little chick. The scenario in their thoughts must have gone something like this. *Hey Bill, what do you think that is?* Bill said, *I don't know Gonzo but it looks like*

a small sea urchin with two big eyes staring out at you. But look at that hair or maybe its feathers I guess, they're sticking straight out from all over its body. Gonzo said, *yeah dig those long knobby legs and that mean, looking beak. Mom and Dad called it, a sparrow or something like that. Maybe I'll go over and tell her how it works at this house. You know, we were here first! What do you think Bill? Sounds good to me,* said Bill, *go on over and straighten her out.* Gonzo came close to her with his beak opened wide trying to intimidate her, that way she would know just who, ruled over the roost! Looking into her eyes he said, *Hi little A. Sparrow, I have something to tell you. I'm Gonzo and I'm the alpha male here and I sort of run things around here.* Before Gonzo could finish, she came jumping out of my hand and ran screaming at Gonzo. *Its, Ms. Sparrow to you, and I'm eating my lunch, so Butt Out!* Gonzo was all wide eyed as he went running off the table and back next to Bill. *Hey Bill, I don't know what she got all bent out of shape about and what did she mean by butt out? I don't know Gonzo* was Bills reply, *but let's give her some space, at least for now. Yeah okay* Gonzo said, *I'll go for that, some space, Uh, maybe just for a few days!* After a few days, everyone was getting along pretty well, but the guys still were not to sure about Ms. Sparrow. However soon we were all on a regular schedule. When it was nappy time, it was quite a sight. Gonzo was on the top of my chest, with me laying down flat on the couch. Bill slept on my shoulder and Ms. Sparrow, still liked to sleep in my cupped right hand. I felt like a big tree lying there as we all snoozed away. The only thing missing was the snoring. My wife said that I snored, but the birds didn't seem to care about it. We were all now like four bugs in a rug.

As the sparrow grew, we wanted her to be able to fly from her cage, and not just down or straight. We felt that she had to show us that she could fly up high with confidence. Each day that passed was full of joy for us, as we watched the little sparrow grow stronger and stronger. After about a week with us my wife took her outside to play in the grass and she really played with gusto. It's fun to watch the birds as they walk or hop around. Bill walks or runs without much body movements, his legs move like he was a windup toy and Gonzo, waddles as he walks. The sparrow, hops all over the place and looks like a furry grasshopper jumping all around the room. When you have this many birds moving around you, you must keep your poop patrol toilet tissue roll, always handy. One of Ms. Sparrow's favorite pastimes was to crawl between the sheets of the tissue roll when it's standing upright. She would shove her way around the inside layers of the roll, until she is about one and a half turns into the outer sheets. It's about there that she would get stuck and had to peck her way through the sidewalls of the tissue. Only her head was sticking out and looking up at you. It's like she was saying, *Peek a Boo, I see you!*

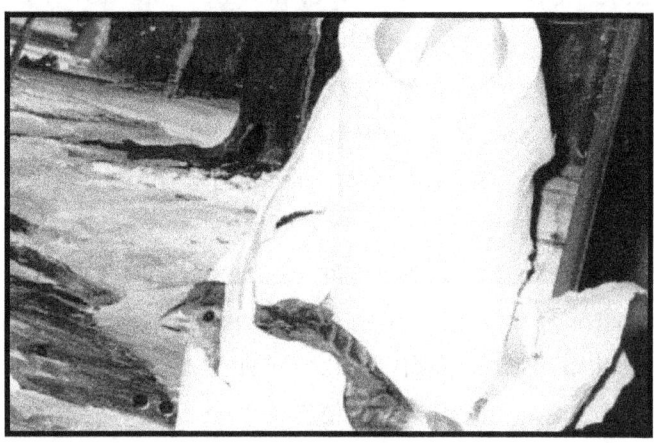

She would hop all around the yard and then into the two small bushes we had in the garden. Finally my wife left her in the bushes all by herself, and all the other sparrows cheeped to her and she came over to the feeding place where they all were eating the seed that we put out in the bird feeder. She got along well with them and I think they knew she was still a chick, because some birds came over to her and showed her how to feed on the seed we had put out. After they all flew away, there she was all by her lonesome. My wife who watched from inside, would go out and bring her back in. All the trees came alive with sounds from all the other sparrows. I guess they were trying to tell her not to go with us. A few days later she could fly better and she flew up to the lower branches and then she would hop up to a higher branch to join the others.

She would stay outside with the others until it started to get dark. Fay would get her feeding bowl and the magic straw that had the spoon on the end of it. When she saw the straw, she flew back down to it. With that, every bird in the trees started again screaming at her. I could only imagine that they were all yelling, hey *don't go, they're people stay here with us!* As you know, all good things must come to an end. One night, she stayed up in the trees with the others and we knew then she was completely raised and now could be on her own. It was a good feeling. But we will always miss her touch. We do see her at the feeding tree and enjoy watching her as she moves among the others, doing what wild birds are supposed to do. Then up with the other birds back with the flock in our spruce trees.

We had her trust when she was young but now the other birds put the fear of man in her. I asked at the wild bird store how you could tell a male sparrow from a female, the clerk said, "The male sparrows have a dark bow tie on their chest and the females don't. I guess that way they're always dressed for a fine dinner! Well how do you like that! I built a long birdhouse and put it under my window awning for the sparrows. It is about four feet long with six different compartments, with a hole for each compartment. Below each hole, I put a suite number, one through six. I call it my Motel 6 and it sure is well used, year after year, hopefully by our little girl, Ms. Sparrow.

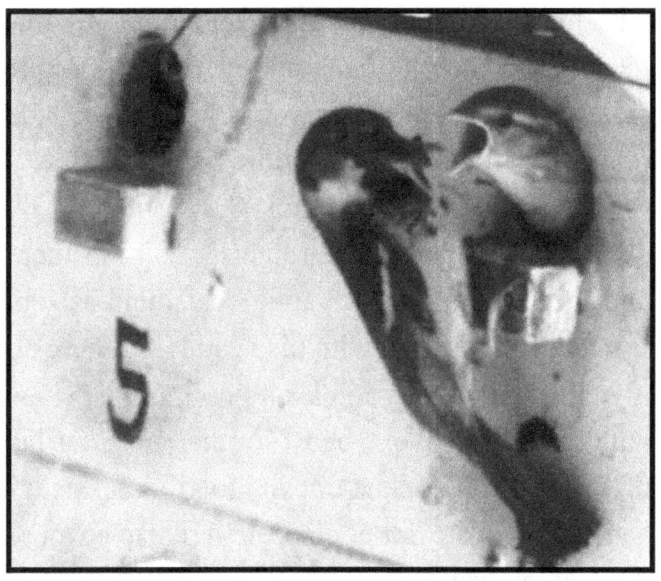

My wife says she still thinks she sees her around from time to time by the window overlooking the birdhouse. I don't know about you, but saving that little life was so rewarding. I think even Bill and Gonzo still miss her from time to time. Ever since we had the sparrow, Gonzo remembers how she liked to sleep in my hand. He now had a big choice ahead of him. Was he going to stay a bit stand offish or did he like the idea Ms. Sparrow had for dad's hand. What to do? It didn't take long before he decided that the hand was to be his! Now he will take my fingers and with his beak, pull them apart, spreading my fingers apart. Then he puts one of his legs on one side of my middle finger, and the other on the other side straddling my middle finger, he slowly moves up and into the crook of my fingers. He almost looks like a green hen just sitting there and then closes his eyes and goes sound asleep. It's funny to see him with his head lying there on my chest tuned to one side and both of his wings hanging down like a baby's arms, snug on his dad's chest, all zonked out and totally at peace! I can't think of any other place he'd like to be more than on my warm, moving chest. I still remember when I needed a black leather glove to get Gonzo out of his cage, and now it's like seeing a small grandchild as he sees me come through the door after work. The minute I enter into the house, he climbs down the cage and runs across the floor to where I'm setting. Up my pants leg all the way up to my chest. After a few brief hello's it's down to the snuggling between my fingers, for as long as I want to hold him. Bill can fly so he usually beats Gonzo over to me and starts talking to me a mile a minute. It's like he's got all this stuff that happened to him all day and now he wants to tell me about it, and right away. Sometimes, Gonzo climbs up onto my wife's chest also for the same comfort and I suspect that he has a mad crush of her. Occasionally he starts to purr like a cat when he's happy. I never knew that birds purred before but he does this for a while and then starts his romance dance. He will sway from side to side and then starts bobbing his head up and down like he's dunking for water. I don't know what to think of this but I'll do the dance with him and he gets that faraway look in his eyes as we both start swaying back and forth and bobbing our heads up and down. I guess the dance means something big time in the bird world.

By now, or daughter Dorothy had moved into a house of her own and we faced a difficult decision as what to do about Bill and Gonzo. Who goes where? Does Gonzo leave our house and go with Dorothy, or does he stay with us? After all, he is her bird, but my wife and I had become attached to Gonzo too. We all felt that the two birds would become very sad and lonely guys if each bird had different homes. After much discussion, we all agreed that the only humane solution was for my wife and I was to keep both birds together at our house. I had hoped deep down for this solution too, but we thought it would only be fair to take them both, to Dorothy's house for visits. So each month we were off in the van to Dorothy's house, some sixty miles away. I was surprised at how well the two boys traveled in their travel cages. We strapped their cages to the back seat for the safety and off we would go. Both guys were happy as clams and every time we went around a curve, they would both lean to the left or the right.

On one of our visits, we were driving down the road, and I made a whistle sound with my lips, and Bill started whistling back to me. Soon Gonzo joined in with the soft whistle sounds he makes in between his loud ack, ack noises that will put a boom box, to shame. Soon the whole van was filled with sound as we all whistled along together. It was almost like a whole gang was singing. "One Hundred Bottles of Beer on the Wall" you know the old driving song where everyone sings as they travel down the road all the way back home. This song went on for almost twenty miles and everyone soon got tired of it all, except Bill. Bill seemed to be having so much fun that he just went on and on. I think he was down to about forty five bottles of beer on the wall when he finally stopped, I guess he hates to sing alone. Can it get any better than this, my friend? I don't think so. The guys took to Dorothy's new house but they were very cautious about all the new things in the room until we were there for a while. As long as you do the things they know they will remain quiet and calm and they stick to you like glue.

You have to make sure all the windows are covered and the fans are off. Birds might fly into a window thinking it's a safe opening and get hurt or be hit by a moving fan blade. Most houses have all these and most likely, even more unknown hazards. So caution is the key word when you have pets as there are many common things you might have around the house that could really hurt them.

We always carry the two birds inside the travel cages with a cover while in the van. You never know what could happen on the road. Even a passing car can frighten birds. This can happen even in the daylight and can send birds flying off into the inside of their cages where they can break a wing. That's what we think happened to Gonzo in the furnace room. Death is a thought that we seldom entertain when we play with our pets, but it's a part of their lives. Animals in the wild live or die each day from all kinds of predators, so with birds, it's fly or die. For them, it's not an easy life. They are often chased by people's dogs or ran over by drivers who have that attitude, "Hey, get out of my way stupid, I'm in a hurry." I'm sure from time to time you have seen that same attitude from other drivers and wished you could see them get theirs. At those times you pray for the police to see them as they drive through the flocks of geese or ducks as they are slowly crossing the roads. All traffic should stop and most will as the wagon train of geese crosses the road. Most all drivers will wait for even the very last one to jump up into the curb to safety. I have wondered to yourself, why don't they just fly over the road, they all have wings? Who knows?

I have been told that geese mate for life, so when the mate is killed, the other one suffers for a long time looking for its own life time mate. To some people, that seems kind of old fashioned, but even the geese have close and long standing family ties. Birds throughout the ages have been finding their way across the country each fall time, and fly back in the spring to their feeding and nesting grounds. All this, without a compass or some mystical GPS around their heads, so there must be some higher intelligence at work that we can only guess at. I'll say it again let's drop the "Just a dumb bird." Give them their due.

As a bus driver, I see more than my share of hurt or dead animals on the road. Because my bus route travels over the same road many times each trip, I must see the road kill over and over. This is no fun for me, so I go out of my way to help those animals get out of harm's way before they go from living creatures to just looking like pieces of paper on the road. Fortunately, most of my days are filled with the beauty that surrounds all of us. Each time I turn the corner, there's another new picture just waiting to be seen.

Mrs. Piper and other Bus Adventures

I'd like to tell you a story about something that happened on one of my new routes I feed the sparrows at the airport each day, and I always carry a small bag of wild birdseed in my pocket. This way I can throw some seed out if I see birds looking around for food at the end of my line. One of my new routes stops by a small pond where there were some ducks and a few Canadian geese milling around. I did my usual thing and dropped some seed by the shore, then went on my way. On my next trip back, I no sooner pulled up and here came the geese. *What a bunch of moochers.* But one bird caught my eye. A single goose was trying to swim from the far side of the pond, but she was having a very hard time of it. She looked as though she was hurt and had to swim using only one leg.

I could see as she swam my way that one of

her wings had been somehow also hurt. When she finally did get to where I had placed out some seed, most of the other birds ran over and made sure it was all quickly eaten. When the others left and it was just, her and I staring at each other, I put what seed I had left on the shore and then had to leave myself.

When I got home, I told my wife about her and what happened. All night, I couldn't get her face out of my mind. The next day on my lunch break, I drove my car over to the pond. I guess I just wanted to see if she was still there. I got out of my car and looked, but all the birds had gone off somewhere. Just then I saw her across the pond coming out of the reeds, heading my way, She was paddling full steam ahead, honking all the way as she tried to paddle toward me. She was swimming so fast she made a visible wake through the water. Who would have thought she would remember me from the day before, but she did. I did notice that as she came my way, she bobbed her head up and down, in some kind of greeting. She did this each time I saw her after that, so it must have been very special to her. Funny thing, I began doing the same to her but made sure no one was around to see me bobbing my head up and down making like a big goose. I still remember when I was in the fabric store, you know, looking for that special cloth for Bill. I didn't want anyone thinking that I was just a nutty bus driver over there by the pond.

I put more seed down and she ate it all up. I could almost see her smile about it. She must have been very hungry because she was looking for more. The pond was located on a street named Piper Lane, near a small airport, so I thought her name should be Mrs. Piper. So that's what I called her from then on. Each day at dusk I would come by and, if all the other birds were there, I had to feed them in one place and her in another otherwise she wouldn't have gotten any food. I discovered that on my way home for lunch was the best time to feed her because all the other birds were off feeding somewhere else.

This went on for about two months and as time passed, I could see her body movements were becoming harder for her. She swam much slower and looked like she was leaning more to one side as she came my way. From what I could see, she had trouble with one wing because it hung down much lower than the other one did.

There was a chill in the air and the leaves were starting to fall. Winter was coming and I become concerned as to how, or if, Mrs. Piper was going to make it through the cold season. Most of the other geese were already starting to fly south.

I mentioned to one of my co-workers about the hurt goose and he said. "Oh I've seen her over on the pond for a couple for years now. She's going to do just fine, don't worry about her." Well, little did I know then that he was lying and really he'd never seen her at all? To him, it was all just foolishness, and said, "A good goose is the one on my plate!" When you talk to killers of birds and not lovers of birds, you soon know that their concerns are not the same as yours, so save your breath my friend. Even when I called the animal rescue and told them about her struggle, there was not much of a response. I was just told that they would look into it. But she only got worse each day and that was really starting to get to me. The next day when I returned for her afternoon feeding,

I didn't see her anywhere. I walked around, listening for her, but heard nothing so I kept walking until I found her. There she was hidden in the high grass along the shoreline, half in and half out of the water. Her right wing had been almost torn off and she was bleeding from the wing joint. There was fresh blood on the rock next to her and I could see that she was in real pain. *Oh God, what do I do, what to do.* She would not let me near her at all she only hissed at me. I really felt helpless and I had to get back to work on time. I called my wife, and told her about Mrs. Piper, how she was hurt, and asked her to please call the rescue people again, I told her that when I got off from work that night, if the animal rescue people didn't come to get her, I was going to somehow catch her myself.

Driving my bus that night was not easy. All I could think about was how did she get hurt so badly? As I thought about it, I came to the conclusion that she must have been laying on the grass by the pond with the other birds, when a worker who was cutting the grass, came along with that "Get out of my way" attitude. I believe in my heart the worker must have driven his grass cutter right through the middle of the flock. He probably thought that all the birds would just fly away as he drove through them all. I guess most of them did, all but Mrs. Piper, with her being hurt, she couldn't move very fast so she was run over and hit by part of his mower. I think that's most likely how one wing was almost about pulled off. I could see that the grass was just freshly mowed.

After my shift was over, I returned back to the pond and after looking all around, I could see that she wasn't there. I started to feel much better then because, that meant that the rescue team had finally came to her aid. On the way home, I prayed that she was going to be okay and felt proud of all my efforts and the efforts of the rescue team. At home, my wife Fay, told me that she had called again that afternoon and was assured that the situation would be taken care of that very night. The next day we stopped by the animal shelter, and we were told that the goose had to be put to sleep because of her extensive injures. I can't tell you how much our hearts were saddened to hear this. Like I said before when someone works with a lot of hurt wild animals, they get used to this sort of thing and can take it in stride. She was just another life form that couldn't be helped and they must move on. But when these creatures become something you get to know, it hits you hard, really deep down. As we left out of the shelter, we passed a small dumpster where the trash was collected I wanted to look inside, but I was afraid to. I just didn't want to see her that way, so quickly gone but never forgotten!

I think that, out of all the wild birds I see each day the geese are one of my favorite. At certain times of the year, they all gather together at a lake my route passes by, and to me, they look like a large herd of buffalo, lazily grazing out on the plains of the Old West. Hundreds and hundreds of geese are all over the place. I know that the workers who take care of the grounds at the parks are not too keen on all the goose droppings, but that's what birds do. One of my passengers calls them, "Dogs with wings," if you know what I mean, I think it's because of all the many poops they leave behind. I enjoy just watching them as they move about, looking for food. When they are all resting on the ground, they have a special majesty about their bodies. If one sleeps the others stand guard to make sure no predators are coming their way. They seem to have a vested interest in each other and when the female is on the nest the male is always close by, that's the trust and that thing called love I talked about in my introduction. Geese mate for life so they must be careful when picking a mate. Like us, if their mate gets killed, they search for a long time for their mate and they then seem to go into, quiet mourning.

I enjoy watching geese, but I couldn't tell you, which one is the male, because from the markings they all look about the same. The answer, I was told is that the males have thicker necks. I guess the geese have no problem with it, so why should I worry. There was a family of geese by the bus barn and I soon got to know the habits of one of the females in the group. Strangely, the others all seemed to ignore her.

She just sat there all alone in the grass under a small tree, while the others ate grass seed and then flew off to other feeding grounds. I couldn't figure out why she was the only one that stayed. This went on for about a week and finally, a male goose came over to her but she spread out her wings and chased him away. I thought to myself, *this girl has an attitude, and she'll never find a mate that way, but she had this look of royalty about her.* Had I given her a name it would have been, "The princess in waiting."

One morning when I came to work, there she was all smiles. Her *"Prince Charming"* had come at last, the two of them both sitting side by side. After all those other handsome guys had tried to court her that week, she had finally got her man. She must have sung those words in beautiful goose talk as she called out for the right male goose. *If it takes forever, I will wait for you,* and then her prince showed up. I guess patience and willingness to wait it out, is really a virtue! I dropped some fresh seed near them both and she was the first to come over to the seed. Strangely enough she did the same head bobbing that Mrs. Piper did. It must mean something in goose talk. I think it maybe means, *we trust you.*

There have been times when I get stuck in traffic and people will ask, "How can you stand driving in this traffic every day, its either a train or it's the weather or something else?"

My answer is, "Each day's an adventure, you never know what the day will bring just deal with it when it shows up." We all seem to be looking or else expecting the big adventure, like the search for Noah's Ark, or searching for the truth, you know…the really big stuff. But, for most of us, life is a bunch of little adventures that seem to rush by each day without us ever even noticing them. You don't have to look for the little adventures each day, they just sort of, show up! Let me tell you about one of mine, one that could have slipped by me, had I not been a bird person. The sun was on the rise and it lit up the clouds with all the colors anyone could ever ask for. I think that God's an early riser because all the trees and buildings stood out from the background, just beautifully. I carefully checked out my bus and made it ready for my morning trips. As I drove to my starting point, I heard the usual rattles and bumps that a bus will make as you drive over the road. Except that I was hearing a much different sound, ever so soft. Chirp, chirp the sound continued. I stopped my bus and carefully listened for any unusual sounds, but the air was quiet, so I drove on my way. However, after a minute I heard the chirps again. *What's going on here, I know I'm a new bird person, but every sound is not coming from a bird.* For the next hour, the sound came and went, but only when I was driving over a bumpy road. I thought maybe some oil would stop the noise. I even asked others on the bus, "Am I hearing things or do any of you hear what I hear? It sounds to me like a bird." All agreed I was not nuts. Sadly for me, none of them thought I had a stowaway bird with me on the bus only a squeaky bus. Each time I stopped the bus the sound would stop. This went on over and over. It became a running joke with everyone as I drove on my route that morning. "You have a big imagination there Chuck, " as each one got off the bus. Everyone would say with a laugh, *"Chip, Chip."* Finally, I was all done with my route and was driving back along to the bus barn. My inner voice said, *I know, what a bird sounds like, and that sound I heard was a bird, I just know it!* Slowly I pulled over at a safe place, I went over to the dashboard of the bus and gave it a hard bang with my hand. Guess what, there was a bird stuck somewhere inside the dashboard of my bus. I carry a small screwdriver on my key chain so I removed some of the screws to the inspection plate, and there he was. A small sparrow stuck way down inside the dash area in the front of the bus. I don't know who was happier, him or me. I reached down and picked him up and held him in my half-closed hand, only his little head was sticking out. He looked like a little sailor with his head sticking out of his private submarine. He seemed quite comfortable as he looked around. He wasn't afraid, just happy to see daylight again. I put him in my shirt pocket and again he seemed very happy. When I got back to the bus barn I showed him to some of the other guys in the garage. We all thought that he had gotten into my bus through one of the holes that the door hinges use, and that he just flew into the hole thinking it was a place to hide. After we all looked him over, I let him go. I believe that his family had made their nest there in the garage and maybe he would be able to stay around the bus barn all year long.

So, you see that was my small adventure that

day. Had I not been the driver of that special bus, at that very special time, and not been a bird person, the bird might have gone unnoticed that day and maybe died inside the bus dashboard.

Who knows, but I feel that fate put me there to do my part and finish my small adventure. This only proves to me that you don't have to look for that very special adventure, they find you, but you have to open your eyes and your minds to them. The way I see it, life is like a big salad bar just waiting for us to help ourselves. However, if we only picked the lettuce each time and never the colorful tomatoes or any of the other tasty things then life would be very boring and not part of the master plan.

I retired in 1999 and friends at my retirement party said to me, "Oh you're just going to go nuts, not having anything to do with your time all day." All I can say to that is I can't wait for all the new adventures that lay ahead for my wife and I and writing these stories about my adventure is just one of them. We have built a small Japanese tea garden in our backyard and find it a nice place to just sit and rest and calmly think about things in general.

I placed a small stone we found on one of our trips out west in the garden where we could see it. Mrs. Piper's name is printed on it, to remind us of her and how her life touched our lives. There are other stones in the garden with other names on them too . Those who sit in these kinds of gardens call these special stones, "familiars." Each time you see them and the names on them, you think about the meaning and the visions they express to us. It's been fun having these guys, Bill, Gonzo, Ms. Sparrow and of course, Mrs. Piper, plus all the other sparrows that came into our lives. When I think about it, our banquet table would be very empty if you could only see the birds off in the distance, and never up close. It's up close that you get to see and know their intelligence and maybe only a small part of the spirit of these other life forms.

While I'm on this subject of animal to human intelligence, let me mention a strange thing that Bill laid on me one day. It came as a complete eye opener to me. Gonzo likes to take a bath in a large pan that I fill up with warm water. He just can't wait to get in and splash around in the water. Bill, on the other hand, won't even go near the water in the pan. One sunny day, the water just sparkled from the sun coming in through the window and Gonzo played in it for a long time. Finally, out he came, dripping wet, but a very happy bird. I turned my head in Bill's direction and said. "Hey, Bill why don't you ever go into the water like Gonzo does, and have some fun. You always sit there and watch Gonzo but never go near the water. How about it Bill, go on down and take a plunge for yourself, it might be fun." Bill looked at me for a moment, and started to walk down my sleeve, then he did something I never thought he would do. He calmly walked into the water and then stood there looking up at me, like he was going to say. *So is that all there is to it, big deal, are you happy now?* With that, he walked back up my sleeve and onto my shoulder and just looked at me. He could see that my mouth was open and that I was speechless, for the first time. He had never and I mean never, walked into water in his life! But he had done what I asked him to do, like he knew what I was saying, I'll never forget that moment in time. Those thoughts and memories are etched in my mind and can be revisited when I look at one of the stones I call a familiar in our Japanese Tea Garden. Each stone has a memory in it.

Up, up and away

It was Sunday and sleeping in was the thing to do. However, the sparrows outside of my window had other thoughts. They had been up early and were busy chirping away while gathering food for the young ones. Off in the distance, I could hear the large black birds barking or cawing to each other, saying just where the morning breakfast was.

I still have trouble thinking about how they get their meals. I guess it's part of all nature, but it's not a pleasant thought while waking up in the morning. The sun was shining through the blinds in my room and the warm, soft breeze of the wind gave me a good feeling as I started to get up and face the day. Have you ever been awake in the morning and said to yourself, *this is going to be a great and really good day?* That's the way I felt that morning, all over my body and in my Spirit that day. It was great to be alive.

My wife was already outside working in the

yard, and Bill and Gonzo were out of their cages. I could hear Bill telling Gonzo, all about his
dreams from last night. When I went into their
room, Gonzo had his head down as though he
was already bored with the whole thing and was
ready to start eating some of Bill's food.

Later that afternoon, I thought it was time to
join my wife in the yard and get some sun. As
I opened the back screen door and stepped out
onto the porch, I felt something hit my shoulder
and bounce off. Moments before, Bill had been
waiting inside near the back door for my wife
to come back in from outside. But I didn't see
him sitting up on the top of the refrigerator as I
passed on by. Out the back door we both went,
me walking, and Bill flying right past my ear.
My "Good day" as it was, is now quickly going
into the blue sky and Bill along with it. Panic
and horror gripped my soul as I saw Bill flying
straight up into the sky. He was screaming loudly
in fright, rising up to about fifty feet into the air
above me. He had never been outside our house
ever since I first found Bill, he was always inside
his cage tucked away safely with Gonzo. To be
outside again on his own was really something

he never expected on that day or any other day. I shouted to my wife that Bill had gotten outside the house and was flying overhead, and telling her that he was heading out over the main highway next to our house. We both started to call up to Bill, trying to get him to come back down to us. Or at least to land somewhere next to or near the house. All we wanted to do was get him safely back home, but only higher he went into the sky. Tears started to roll down both our faces as we ran along the highway, pleading with Bill to come down. We feared that he would fly about a mile down the road before he came down and maybe then would be lost forever. The sound of our voices calling to him kept him over the road where we could see him. I know he could hear our sobbing cries. Bill's panicky screams are like a police whistle, high pitched and shrill. We knew this is the sound Bill makes when he doesn't see us when he flies into the bathroom and then thinks he's lost.

Everything around him now was scary and unfamiliar to him. So there we were, all three of us calling out to each other, you could hear the sheer panic in our voices. Bill saying, *Help I'm lost* and us sobbing, "Oh God, Bill, please come back home to us." We knew that when housebound pet birds get away, they don't know where they are in the outside world. All they ever see is the inside of our house and that's where it is safe to be. It is very frightful for them when they are outside. The highway that passes by our house is very fast moving and has a lot of trucks speeding along, plus all the traffic nose. I suppose it was like this when Bill first came to us after being lost seven years ago. Yes. We have had Bill that long and then to lose him now, well you know how that would feel. Not seeing him again would be more than we could take. He flew up and down over the highway, coming down to just above the road. I could see that he was quickly getting tired very fast. One car in the speeding traffic saw him and slowed down trying to avoid hitting him or even worse, running him over. I think seeing that would have torn our hearts out, right there on the spot. It's something you would never forget or get over. The time passed as though it was being marked in slow motion and that I was moving to slow to ever catch him. My words just dribbled out of my mouth as I call to him, "Oh Bill come back." As I ran, I had flashes of him flying far away, and then being torn apart by some crows or by a cat. These thoughts all raced through my mind as I ran. Bill trusted other people and animals, so I believe he would be easy prey out there in the wild. The sheer terror of it all made me cry even more. *What about Gonzo?* He and Bill had become close partners through the many years and he would be all by himself again. It would be a lot of loneliness for all of us. I felt complete helplessness and asked God again to send him back to us. At those times, you kind of get carried away with the many promises you make with God. You know, if you give me what I'm asking for, I'll do this or that. Anything… you just tell me what you want and it's yours God, It's yours! All this time bill is still flying all over the place, toward us one minute, then away from us. I'm sure the people driving their cars were wondering, just what are those two crazy people doing waving their arms into the air and screaming up into the sky. Maybe it is a rain dance, or that we were high on something, who knows. Then it happened!

In one low power dive, Bill swooped down into our backyard. We ran as fast as our legs could go all the way behind to the garage and there was Bill, clinging to the chain-link fence and among the flowers. His eyes were almost as big as mine were and he was screaming at the top of his lungs for someone to come and get him, and I mean, right now! The feathers on the top of his head were standing straight up and his chest was just a pumping away. I went over to him and with my hand cupped, I picked him up and pressed him to my chest and then into my jacket where he would be safe. He didn't even move when I kissed his head and I kind of think he had a smile of his face. He was home. Our prayers were answered that day so I know I have a big I.O U. with the guy up stairs, big time. We all went back inside the house and just sat on the couch for a long time wiping our eyes saying, "Oh Bill you scared us so much, so much." We could tell that he was thinking about what had happened to him because he was very quiet for a few days after his big adventure. I guess it was ours too, now he never goes near a door.

Bill came to us a free bird, and we had never

trimmed his flight wing feathers before. We were going on a vacation in a few days so we had to make the call to trim his flight feathers or not. Trimming the tips of their flight wing feathers does not hurt the bird, but it will only let them fly a few feet away from you. That way they are easy to catch again. Most pet shops and pet owners who have birds can learn to trim the feathers safely with no harm to their birds. The time to trim Bill's feathers had come, so off to the vets we went. Bill is a fast flyer so he was very quiet for a few days until he figured that it was more fun to have us pick him up and carry him from one room to another. I think he now considers us, his own private slaves. Now, he had to walk around the house like Gonzo does or wait for us to come to get him. This part of my adventure I don't want to do again. We have had a lot of fun with our birds over the years and I even made a Christmas card with a picture of Gonzo on the front of it and sent it as a thank you note to his doctor. That really went over big at the doctor's office. Gonzo is a handsome man bird and I often do tell him that he is. This I could see by his eyes made him a very happy boy. Before I close the story about my bird adventures, I'd like to leave you with a few thoughts as I see them.

Like I said in my introduction, trust and fate I feel are the fine threads that binds most happy lives together and without that trust few of my adventures could have been done. Had Bill not trusted, he would not have let me pick him up the first time, he would have flown away and had Gonzo not learned to trust us he would have clung to the side of his cage and just screamed at us. He never would have understood the love that grew very strong between him and our family and he would have stayed an unhappy bird and very lonesome by himself. They trusted us and finally felt the love we had to give them. I feel they all trusted us and fate brought us all together. I am honored to have met them all.

Generations of people have often looked up to the skies, hoping to meet a new alien life form from another faraway planet landing here on earth. Science fiction movies show us all kinds of strange creatures, with big buggy eyes and antennas coming out of their heads. Others have arms with monster claws attached to them and they have odd, looking faces that only a mother crab could love. We all know from those movies that they are here only, to capture us and place us humans in cages for observation. In the movies, when they're all done scaring us half to death, we finally fight them off and just before they eat us up, maybe we eat them up first.

It's funny, but you know, I think I've seen some of those strange looking life forms running around in my garden outside or they are roaming around in our forests and lakes. One day, in the local pond, I found those same guys with the big claws, just swimming or walking around on the bottom *Hmmm*. After giving this some thought, I said to myself, *wait a minute! Maybe to them, we're really the alien extra-terrestrials and, to a small crab, we're just plain ugly, and that's with a capital U.* What I see is a lot of animals who were really here first, so stop looking way out there. The other life forms are not somewhere else, they're right here, next to and all around us! We are also, part of the *family* of all life! Was it fate that bought Bill to us? I think we are all fully connected to nature and with all its other life forms too, which by the way includes us. All parts of nature should be important to us. Some people consider animals only "things." Those of you who have, or have had loving pets know what I'm saying. I really feel there must be a force out there directing us all together as we all move along in this life. I hope that in the hereafter that we will all meet again, and get to do it all over again.

God does love us all, and that includes the birds too, because as the scriptures tell us. "Not even a sparrow falls from the sky without God knowing about it." So I guess if it's important to him, then it should also be important to us too. You've read about my adventure, now start one of your own. Like, Bill, I'm about all talked out, so my final words to all of you bird and animal lovers on earths beautiful space ship is – "Now listen up all you Junior Birdmen. This is your commander speaking to you from the bridge. We have landed, go explore, respect and enjoy what you see . . . just don't invade."

THE END

Acknowledgments

I would like to thank my wife Fay and my daughter Dorothy, for their support while writing this book. There were many doubtful moments in this creation and they gave me the moral support I needed to finish writing about my adventures and to never give up.

Thanks to the many passengers that rode my bus and exchanged stories about their pets. My bus became the happy bus when people got to talk about all the pets that they loved. It was fun and a good way to make new friends with happy faces.

To my loving friends Gonzo and Bill who have passed away while I was writing their stories. I could not express the sadness we felt about this because it brought much sorrow to our family. I could not include this in my stories because I always would become too emotional when I thought about them, sorry.

I would also like to thank Tina, Sara, and the Production crew at Outskirt Press, for guiding me through the many problems that come with publishing a book by a new author.

Thanks to you all.